50 Sweet Treats and Dessert Recipes

By: Kelly Johnson

Table of Contents

- Chocolate Lava Cake
- Tiramisu
- Cheesecake
- Brownies
- Lemon Meringue Pie
- Apple Crumble
- Key Lime Pie
- Cupcakes
- Chocolate Chip Cookies
- Macarons
- Pavlova
- Fruit Tart
- Banana Pudding
- Cream Puffs
- Rice Pudding
- Eclairs
- Crème Brûlée
- Baklava
- Panna Cotta
- Churros
- Cannoli
- Gelato
- S'mores
- Coconut Macaroons
- Ice Cream Sundae
- Sticky Toffee Pudding
- Peanut Butter Pie
- Carrot Cake
- Chocolate Truffles
- Pecan Pie
- Raspberry Sorbet
- Strawberry Shortcake
- Flourless Chocolate Cake
- Profiteroles
- Chocolate Mousse

- Salted Caramel Brownies
- Mint Chocolate Chip Ice Cream
- Pumpkin Pie
- Almond Cake
- Lemon Bars
- Fruit Sorbet
- Chocolate Dipped Strawberries
- Fudge
- White Chocolate Raspberry Cheesecake
- Snickerdoodle Cookies
- Oatmeal Raisin Cookies
- Chocoflan
- Toffee Pudding
- Coconut Cream Pie
- Spiced Pear Cake

Chocolate Lava Cake

Ingredients:

- 1/2 cup unsalted butter
- 6 oz semi-sweet chocolate
- 1/2 cup powdered sugar
- 2 whole eggs
- 2 egg yolks
- 1 teaspoon vanilla extract
- 1/4 cup all-purpose flour
- A pinch of salt
- Butter and cocoa powder for greasing ramekins

Instructions:

1. Preheat the oven to 425°F (220°C). Butter and dust four ramekins with cocoa powder.
2. Melt the butter and chocolate together in a heatproof bowl over simmering water, stirring until smooth.
3. Whisk the powdered sugar, eggs, egg yolks, and vanilla into the melted chocolate mixture until smooth.
4. Fold in the flour and salt, then pour the batter evenly into the prepared ramekins.
5. Bake for 12-14 minutes, until the edges are set but the center is soft.
6. Let the cakes rest for 1 minute, then carefully invert onto plates and serve with vanilla ice cream or whipped cream.

Tiramisu

Ingredients:

- 1 cup brewed espresso, cooled
- 1/2 cup rum or coffee liqueur (optional)
- 24 ladyfingers
- 1 cup mascarpone cheese
- 1 cup heavy cream
- 1/2 cup powdered sugar
- 1 teaspoon vanilla extract
- Cocoa powder for dusting
- Dark chocolate shavings (optional)

Instructions:

1. Mix the espresso and rum (if using) in a shallow dish.
2. Dip the ladyfingers into the espresso mixture for 1-2 seconds, then layer them in the bottom of a dish.
3. In a large bowl, whisk together mascarpone, heavy cream, powdered sugar, and vanilla until smooth and thick.
4. Spread half of the mascarpone mixture over the ladyfingers, then repeat with another layer of dipped ladyfingers and the remaining mascarpone mixture.
5. Cover and refrigerate for at least 4 hours, or overnight.
6. Before serving, dust with cocoa powder and garnish with chocolate shavings.

Cheesecake

Ingredients:

- 1 1/2 cups graham cracker crumbs
- 1/4 cup sugar
- 1/2 cup melted butter
- 4 (8 oz) packages cream cheese, softened
- 1 cup granulated sugar
- 1 teaspoon vanilla extract
- 4 large eggs
- 1 cup sour cream
- 1/4 cup heavy cream

Instructions:

1. Preheat the oven to 325°F (163°C).
2. Mix graham cracker crumbs, sugar, and melted butter, then press into the bottom of a springform pan to form the crust. Bake for 10 minutes and set aside.
3. Beat the cream cheese, granulated sugar, and vanilla in a large bowl until smooth.
4. Add eggs, one at a time, beating well after each addition.
5. Stir in sour cream and heavy cream until smooth.
6. Pour the batter over the crust and bake for 50-60 minutes, until the center is set.
7. Cool completely, then refrigerate for at least 4 hours before serving.

Brownies

Ingredients:

- 1/2 cup unsalted butter
- 8 oz semi-sweet chocolate
- 3/4 cup granulated sugar
- 1/2 cup brown sugar
- 3 large eggs
- 1 teaspoon vanilla extract
- 1/2 cup all-purpose flour
- 1/4 teaspoon salt
- 1/4 teaspoon baking powder

Instructions:

1. Preheat the oven to 350°F (175°C). Grease and line a baking pan.
2. Melt the butter and chocolate together in a saucepan over low heat, stirring constantly until smooth.
3. Stir in the sugars, eggs, and vanilla extract.
4. Add the flour, salt, and baking powder, and mix until just combined.
5. Pour the batter into the prepared pan and bake for 20-25 minutes, until a toothpick inserted into the center comes out with a few moist crumbs.
6. Let cool before cutting into squares.

Lemon Meringue Pie

Ingredients:

- 1 pie crust (store-bought or homemade)
- 1 1/4 cups granulated sugar
- 1/4 cup cornstarch
- 1/4 teaspoon salt
- 1 1/2 cups water
- 3 large egg yolks, beaten
- 1/2 cup fresh lemon juice
- 2 teaspoons lemon zest
- 1 tablespoon unsalted butter
- 3 large egg whites
- 1/4 teaspoon cream of tartar
- 6 tablespoons granulated sugar

Instructions:

1. Preheat the oven to 350°F (175°C). Blind bake the pie crust for 10 minutes and set aside.
2. In a saucepan, combine sugar, cornstarch, salt, and water. Bring to a boil, stirring constantly until thickened.
3. Whisk a small amount of the hot mixture into the egg yolks, then return to the saucepan, stirring constantly.
4. Stir in lemon juice, zest, and butter, then pour the filling into the baked crust.
5. Beat the egg whites and cream of tartar until soft peaks form, then gradually add sugar and beat until stiff peaks form.
6. Spread the meringue over the lemon filling and bake for 10-12 minutes, until golden.
7. Cool completely before serving.

Apple Crumble

Ingredients:

- 4 apples, peeled, cored, and sliced
- 1 tablespoon lemon juice
- 1/2 cup granulated sugar
- 1 teaspoon cinnamon
- 1/2 cup all-purpose flour
- 1/4 cup rolled oats
- 1/4 cup brown sugar
- 1/4 cup unsalted butter, cubed
- Pinch of salt

Instructions:

1. Preheat the oven to 375°F (190°C).
2. Toss the apple slices with lemon juice, granulated sugar, and cinnamon. Place in a greased baking dish.
3. In a separate bowl, combine the flour, oats, brown sugar, and salt. Cut in the butter until the mixture resembles coarse crumbs.
4. Sprinkle the crumble topping evenly over the apples.
5. Bake for 35-40 minutes, until the apples are tender and the topping is golden brown.

Key Lime Pie

Ingredients:

- 1 1/2 cups graham cracker crumbs
- 1/4 cup granulated sugar
- 1/2 cup unsalted butter, melted
- 3/4 cup fresh lime juice
- Zest of 2 limes
- 1 (14 oz) can sweetened condensed milk
- 3 large egg yolks
- Whipped cream for topping

Instructions:

1. Preheat the oven to 350°F (175°C).
2. Mix the graham cracker crumbs, sugar, and melted butter, then press into the bottom of a pie dish.
3. Bake the crust for 10 minutes, then let it cool.
4. In a bowl, whisk together lime juice, lime zest, sweetened condensed milk, and egg yolks.
5. Pour the filling into the cooled crust and bake for 15-20 minutes until set.
6. Cool to room temperature, then refrigerate for at least 2 hours.
7. Top with whipped cream before serving.

Cupcakes

Ingredients:

- 1 1/2 cups all-purpose flour
- 1 1/2 teaspoons baking powder
- 1/4 teaspoon salt
- 1/2 cup unsalted butter, softened
- 1 cup granulated sugar
- 2 large eggs
- 1 teaspoon vanilla extract
- 1/2 cup milk
- Frosting of your choice (buttercream, cream cheese, etc.)

Instructions:

1. Preheat the oven to 350°F (175°C) and line a cupcake tin with paper liners.
2. Whisk together flour, baking powder, and salt.
3. Cream the butter and sugar together until light and fluffy. Add eggs one at a time, then stir in vanilla.
4. Gradually add the dry ingredients in batches, alternating with milk, until fully combined.
5. Divide the batter evenly into the cupcake liners and bake for 18-20 minutes.
6. Cool completely before frosting.

Chocolate Chip Cookies

Ingredients:

- 2 1/4 cups all-purpose flour
- 1/2 teaspoon baking soda
- 1 cup unsalted butter, softened
- 1/2 cup granulated sugar
- 1 cup brown sugar, packed
- 2 teaspoons vanilla extract
- 2 large eggs
- 2 cups semisweet chocolate chips
- 1/2 teaspoon salt

Instructions:

1. Preheat the oven to 375°F (190°C). Line a baking sheet with parchment paper.
2. In a bowl, whisk together flour, baking soda, and salt.
3. Beat butter, granulated sugar, brown sugar, and vanilla extract until creamy. Add eggs one at a time.
4. Gradually add the dry ingredients, mixing until combined.
5. Stir in chocolate chips.
6. Drop rounded tablespoons of dough onto the baking sheet, leaving space between each cookie.
7. Bake for 9-11 minutes, until golden brown around the edges. Let cool on a wire rack.

Macarons

Ingredients:

- 1 1/2 cups powdered sugar
- 1 cup almond flour
- 2 large egg whites
- 1/4 teaspoon cream of tartar
- 1/4 cup granulated sugar
- 1 teaspoon vanilla extract
- Buttercream or jam for filling

Instructions:

1. Preheat the oven to 300°F (150°C) and line a baking sheet with parchment paper.
2. Sift together powdered sugar and almond flour.
3. Beat egg whites and cream of tartar until soft peaks form, then gradually add granulated sugar and beat until stiff peaks form.
4. Gently fold the dry ingredients into the meringue until smooth.
5. Pipe the batter onto the baking sheet in small circles. Let them sit for 30 minutes to form a skin.
6. Bake for 15-18 minutes, then cool completely.
7. Sandwich with buttercream or jam.

Pavlova

Ingredients:

- 4 large egg whites
- 1 cup granulated sugar
- 1 teaspoon vanilla extract
- 1 teaspoon white vinegar
- 1 tablespoon cornstarch
- Fresh fruit (berries, kiwi, etc.)
- Whipped cream for topping

Instructions:

1. Preheat the oven to 250°F (120°C). Line a baking sheet with parchment paper.
2. Beat egg whites until soft peaks form, then gradually add sugar, vanilla, vinegar, and cornstarch. Beat until stiff peaks form.
3. Spoon the meringue onto the prepared baking sheet into a round shape with a slight dip in the center.
4. Bake for 1 hour, then turn off the oven and let the pavlova cool completely inside the oven.
5. Top with whipped cream and fresh fruit before serving.

Fruit Tart

Ingredients:

- 1 pre-made tart shell or homemade shortcrust pastry
- 1 1/4 cups heavy cream
- 1/2 cup mascarpone cheese
- 1/4 cup powdered sugar
- 1 teaspoon vanilla extract
- Assorted fresh fruits (berries, kiwi, mango, etc.)
- Apricot jam (for glaze)

Instructions:

1. Preheat the oven to 350°F (175°C). If using homemade pastry, roll it out and fit it into a tart pan. Blind bake the crust for about 10-12 minutes until golden. Let cool.
2. Whisk together heavy cream, mascarpone, powdered sugar, and vanilla extract until soft peaks form.
3. Fill the cooled tart shell with the mascarpone cream mixture.
4. Arrange fresh fruit on top of the cream.
5. Warm apricot jam and brush it over the fruit to give it a glossy finish.
6. Refrigerate until ready to serve.

Banana Pudding

Ingredients:

- 2 cups milk
- 1/2 cup sugar
- 1/3 cup cornstarch
- 1/4 teaspoon salt
- 3 large egg yolks
- 1 teaspoon vanilla extract
- 1 1/2 cups heavy cream
- 2 ripe bananas, sliced
- 1 package vanilla wafers

Instructions:

1. In a saucepan, whisk together milk, sugar, cornstarch, and salt. Bring to a simmer over medium heat, whisking constantly until thickened.
2. In a separate bowl, whisk egg yolks and slowly add a small amount of the hot milk mixture to temper them. Pour the egg mixture into the saucepan and cook for 2-3 more minutes.
3. Remove from heat and stir in vanilla extract.
4. In a serving dish, layer the vanilla wafers, sliced bananas, and custard. Repeat the layers.
5. Whip the heavy cream to stiff peaks and spread it over the top of the pudding.
6. Refrigerate for at least 4 hours before serving.

Cream Puffs

Ingredients:

- 1 cup water
- 1/2 cup unsalted butter
- 1 cup all-purpose flour
- 1/4 teaspoon salt
- 4 large eggs
- 1 cup heavy cream
- 2 tablespoons powdered sugar
- 1 teaspoon vanilla extract

Instructions:

1. Preheat the oven to 400°F (200°C). Line a baking sheet with parchment paper.
2. In a saucepan, bring water and butter to a boil. Stir in flour and salt until the mixture pulls away from the sides of the pan.
3. Remove from heat and add eggs, one at a time, beating after each addition until smooth.
4. Drop tablespoon-sized mounds of dough onto the prepared baking sheet.
5. Bake for 20-25 minutes, until puffed and golden. Let cool.
6. Whip the heavy cream with powdered sugar and vanilla until stiff peaks form.
7. Slice each cream puff in half and fill with whipped cream.

Rice Pudding

Ingredients:

- 1 cup Arborio rice
- 4 cups whole milk
- 1/2 cup sugar
- 1 teaspoon vanilla extract
- 1/2 teaspoon ground cinnamon
- 1/4 teaspoon salt
- 1 tablespoon butter (optional)

Instructions:

1. In a saucepan, bring the milk to a simmer over medium heat. Add the rice, sugar, cinnamon, and salt.
2. Stir occasionally and cook for 20-25 minutes, until the rice is tender and the mixture thickens.
3. Remove from heat and stir in vanilla extract and butter.
4. Let the pudding cool to room temperature or refrigerate to serve chilled.

Eclairs

Ingredients:

- 1 cup water
- 1/2 cup unsalted butter
- 1 cup all-purpose flour
- 1/4 teaspoon salt
- 4 large eggs
- 1 cup heavy cream
- 1/4 cup powdered sugar
- 1 teaspoon vanilla extract
- 4 oz semisweet chocolate, chopped

Instructions:

1. Preheat the oven to 400°F (200°C). Line a baking sheet with parchment paper.
2. In a saucepan, bring water and butter to a boil. Stir in flour and salt until the mixture forms a ball.
3. Remove from heat and add eggs one at a time, mixing well after each addition.
4. Pipe the dough into 3-inch long strips on the prepared baking sheet.
5. Bake for 20-25 minutes until puffed and golden. Let cool.
6. Whip the heavy cream with powdered sugar and vanilla until stiff peaks form.
7. Slice each eclair in half, fill with whipped cream, and drizzle with melted chocolate.

Crème Brûlée

Ingredients:

- 2 cups heavy cream
- 1 vanilla bean, split (or 2 teaspoons vanilla extract)
- 5 large egg yolks
- 1/2 cup granulated sugar
- 2 tablespoons light brown sugar (for topping)

Instructions:

1. Preheat the oven to 325°F (163°C). Place 4 ramekins in a baking dish.
2. In a saucepan, heat the heavy cream with the vanilla bean (or extract) until simmering. Remove from heat and let steep for 10 minutes.
3. In a separate bowl, whisk egg yolks and granulated sugar until pale and thick.
4. Gradually pour the warm cream into the egg mixture, whisking constantly to avoid curdling.
5. Strain the mixture through a fine mesh sieve into a clean bowl.
6. Pour the custard into the ramekins and place the baking dish in the oven. Fill the dish with hot water halfway up the sides of the ramekins.
7. Bake for 45-50 minutes until set but still slightly wobbly in the center.
8. Cool, then refrigerate for at least 2 hours.
9. Before serving, sprinkle brown sugar on top and caramelize with a kitchen torch.

Baklava

Ingredients:

- 1 package phyllo dough
- 2 cups mixed nuts (walnuts, pistachios, almonds), chopped
- 1 cup unsalted butter, melted
- 1 teaspoon ground cinnamon
- 1 cup granulated sugar
- 1 cup water
- 1/2 cup honey
- 1 teaspoon vanilla extract

Instructions:

1. Preheat the oven to 350°F (175°C). Brush a baking dish with melted butter.
2. Layer 8 sheets of phyllo dough, brushing each sheet with butter. Sprinkle a thin layer of chopped nuts and cinnamon.
3. Continue layering phyllo and nuts until the dish is full, finishing with a final 8 layers of phyllo dough.
4. Cut the baklava into diamond shapes.
5. Bake for 45-50 minutes until golden and crisp.
6. In a saucepan, combine sugar, water, honey, and vanilla extract. Bring to a simmer and cook for 10 minutes.
7. Pour the syrup over the hot baklava and let cool completely before serving.

Panna Cotta

Ingredients:

- 2 cups heavy cream
- 1/2 cup whole milk
- 1/2 cup sugar
- 1 teaspoon vanilla extract
- 2 1/4 teaspoons unflavored gelatin
- 3 tablespoons water

Instructions:

1. In a small bowl, sprinkle the gelatin over the water and let it bloom for 5 minutes.
2. In a saucepan, heat the cream, milk, and sugar until warm but not boiling. Stir until the sugar dissolves.
3. Remove from heat and stir in the bloomed gelatin and vanilla extract until fully dissolved.
4. Pour the mixture into individual molds or ramekins.
5. Refrigerate for at least 4 hours or overnight until set.
6. To serve, run a knife around the edges and invert onto plates. Serve with fruit compote or berries.

Churros

Ingredients:

- 1 cup water
- 2 tablespoons granulated sugar
- 1/2 teaspoon salt
- 2 tablespoons unsalted butter
- 1 cup all-purpose flour
- 2 large eggs
- 1/2 teaspoon vanilla extract
- 1/4 cup cinnamon-sugar (for coating)

Instructions:

1. In a saucepan, bring water, sugar, salt, and butter to a boil.
2. Stir in the flour until the dough forms a ball. Remove from heat and let cool slightly.
3. Beat in eggs one at a time, then stir in vanilla extract.
4. Heat oil in a deep fryer or large pot to 375°F (190°C).
5. Pipe the dough into the hot oil in long strips and fry until golden and crispy, about 2-3 minutes.
6. Drain on paper towels, then roll in cinnamon-sugar.
7. Serve warm.

Cannoli

Ingredients:

- 1 package cannoli shells
- 2 cups ricotta cheese, drained
- 1 cup powdered sugar
- 1 teaspoon vanilla extract
- 1/2 teaspoon ground cinnamon
- 1/2 cup mini chocolate chips (optional)
- Pistachios, chopped (optional)

Instructions:

1. In a bowl, mix ricotta, powdered sugar, vanilla, and cinnamon until smooth.
2. Fill the cannoli shells with the ricotta mixture using a piping bag.
3. Optionally, dip the ends in mini chocolate chips or chopped pistachios.
4. Serve immediately, or refrigerate for up to 2 hours before serving.

Gelato

Ingredients:

- 2 cups whole milk
- 1 cup heavy cream
- 3/4 cup granulated sugar
- 1 teaspoon vanilla extract
- 4 large egg yolks

Instructions:

1. In a saucepan, heat the milk and cream until warm but not boiling. Remove from heat.
2. In a bowl, whisk together the sugar and egg yolks until light and fluffy.
3. Slowly add the warm milk mixture to the egg yolks, whisking constantly.
4. Pour the mixture back into the saucepan and cook over low heat, stirring constantly until it thickens (coats the back of a spoon).
5. Remove from heat, stir in vanilla extract, and let the mixture cool completely.
6. Pour the cooled mixture into an ice cream maker and churn according to the manufacturer's instructions.
7. Once churned, transfer to a container and freeze for at least 4 hours before serving.

S'mores

Ingredients:

- 1 pack graham crackers
- 4 large marshmallows
- 2 milk chocolate bars

Instructions:

1. Toast marshmallows over an open flame or in the oven until golden brown and gooey.
2. Break graham crackers in half to form squares.
3. Place a piece of chocolate on a graham cracker square, top with a toasted marshmallow, and close with another graham cracker square.
4. Serve warm and enjoy the gooey goodness.

Coconut Macaroons

Ingredients:

- 2 1/2 cups shredded coconut
- 1 cup sweetened condensed milk
- 1/4 teaspoon vanilla extract
- 2 egg whites
- 1/4 teaspoon salt

Instructions:

1. Preheat oven to 325°F (163°C). Line a baking sheet with parchment paper.
2. In a large bowl, combine the coconut, sweetened condensed milk, and vanilla extract.
3. In a separate bowl, beat egg whites and salt until stiff peaks form.
4. Gently fold the egg whites into the coconut mixture until combined.
5. Scoop spoonfuls of the mixture onto the prepared baking sheet.
6. Bake for 15-20 minutes, or until golden brown. Let cool completely before serving.

Ice Cream Sundae

Ingredients:

- 3 scoops of your favorite ice cream (chocolate, vanilla, or strawberry)
- Chocolate syrup
- Whipped cream
- Chopped nuts (optional)
- Maraschino cherry

Instructions:

1. Place three scoops of ice cream in a bowl or sundae dish.
2. Drizzle with chocolate syrup.
3. Top with whipped cream, chopped nuts, and a maraschino cherry.
4. Serve immediately and enjoy.

Sticky Toffee Pudding

Ingredients:

- 1 1/2 cups pitted dates, chopped
- 1 teaspoon baking soda
- 1 1/2 cups boiling water
- 1/2 cup unsalted butter, softened
- 1 cup brown sugar
- 2 large eggs
- 1 1/2 cups all-purpose flour
- 1 teaspoon baking powder
- 1/4 teaspoon salt
- 1 teaspoon vanilla extract
- 1 cup heavy cream
- 1/4 cup dark brown sugar

Instructions:

1. Preheat oven to 350°F (175°C). Grease a baking dish.
2. In a bowl, combine chopped dates and baking soda. Pour boiling water over the dates and let sit for 10 minutes.
3. In another bowl, cream together butter and brown sugar. Add eggs and beat until smooth.
4. In a separate bowl, whisk together flour, baking powder, and salt. Gradually add this mixture to the wet ingredients, mixing until combined.
5. Stir in the date mixture (including liquid) and vanilla extract.
6. Pour the batter into the prepared baking dish and bake for 30-35 minutes.
7. In a saucepan, heat heavy cream and dark brown sugar until melted and smooth. Pour over the baked pudding.
8. Serve warm with extra toffee sauce.

Peanut Butter Pie

Ingredients:

- 1 graham cracker crust
- 1 cup creamy peanut butter
- 8 oz cream cheese, softened
- 1 cup powdered sugar
- 1 cup heavy cream
- 1 teaspoon vanilla extract
- 1/4 cup chocolate chips (optional)

Instructions:

1. In a bowl, beat together peanut butter, cream cheese, and powdered sugar until smooth.
2. In a separate bowl, whip the heavy cream and vanilla extract until stiff peaks form.
3. Gently fold the whipped cream into the peanut butter mixture.
4. Pour the filling into the graham cracker crust and smooth the top.
5. Refrigerate for at least 4 hours before serving.
6. Optionally, drizzle with melted chocolate and sprinkle with chocolate chips before serving.

Carrot Cake

Ingredients:

- 2 cups all-purpose flour
- 1 1/2 teaspoons baking powder
- 1 teaspoon baking soda
- 1 teaspoon ground cinnamon
- 1/2 teaspoon ground nutmeg
- 1/2 teaspoon salt
- 1 1/2 cups granulated sugar
- 1/2 cup vegetable oil
- 4 large eggs
- 2 cups grated carrots
- 1/2 cup crushed walnuts (optional)

Instructions:

1. Preheat oven to 350°F (175°C). Grease and flour two 9-inch round cake pans.
2. In a bowl, whisk together flour, baking powder, baking soda, cinnamon, nutmeg, and salt.
3. In a separate bowl, beat together sugar, oil, and eggs until smooth.
4. Stir in grated carrots and walnuts (if using).
5. Gradually add the dry ingredients to the wet mixture, mixing until combined.
6. Pour the batter into the prepared pans and bake for 30-35 minutes, or until a toothpick inserted comes out clean.
7. Let the cakes cool completely, then frost with cream cheese frosting and serve.

Chocolate Truffles

Ingredients:

- 8 oz semisweet chocolate, chopped
- 1/2 cup heavy cream
- 1/2 teaspoon vanilla extract
- Cocoa powder (for rolling)

Instructions:

1. In a saucepan, heat heavy cream until simmering. Pour over chopped chocolate and let sit for 5 minutes.
2. Stir the mixture until smooth and glossy. Add vanilla extract and mix.
3. Let the ganache cool to room temperature, then refrigerate for 2-3 hours until firm.
4. Scoop the ganache into small balls and roll in cocoa powder.
5. Refrigerate the truffles until ready to serve.

Pecan Pie

Ingredients:

- 1 pre-made pie crust
- 1 1/2 cups pecan halves
- 3/4 cup light corn syrup
- 3/4 cup brown sugar
- 3 large eggs
- 1/4 cup unsalted butter, melted
- 1 teaspoon vanilla extract
- 1/4 teaspoon salt

Instructions:

1. Preheat oven to 350°F (175°C). Place pie crust in a pie dish.
2. In a bowl, whisk together corn syrup, brown sugar, eggs, melted butter, vanilla, and salt.
3. Stir in the pecans and pour the filling into the pie crust.
4. Bake for 45-50 minutes until the center is set.
5. Let the pie cool completely before serving.

Raspberry Sorbet

Ingredients:

- 4 cups fresh raspberries
- 1 cup granulated sugar
- 1 cup water
- 1 tablespoon lemon juice

Instructions:

1. In a saucepan, combine sugar and water. Heat over medium heat until the sugar dissolves.
2. In a blender, puree the raspberries and strain to remove seeds.
3. Stir the raspberry puree into the sugar syrup and add lemon juice.
4. Pour the mixture into an ice cream maker and churn according to the manufacturer's instructions.
5. Freeze for 2-3 hours before serving.

Strawberry Shortcake

Ingredients:

- 2 cups fresh strawberries, sliced
- 1/4 cup granulated sugar
- 1 1/2 cups all-purpose flour
- 2 teaspoons baking powder
- 1/2 teaspoon salt
- 1/4 cup cold unsalted butter, cubed
- 2/3 cup heavy cream
- Whipped cream for topping

Instructions:

1. Toss the sliced strawberries with sugar and let sit for 30 minutes to release juices.
2. Preheat oven to 400°F (200°C). In a bowl, combine flour, baking powder, and salt.
3. Cut in the cold butter until the mixture resembles coarse crumbs.
4. Add heavy cream and stir until the dough comes together.
5. Turn the dough out onto a floured surface, knead lightly, and roll out to 1-inch thickness. Cut into circles.
6. Place on a baking sheet and bake for 12-15 minutes, or until golden.
7. To serve, split the shortcakes in half, top with strawberries, and add whipped cream.

Flourless Chocolate Cake

Ingredients:

- 8 oz bittersweet or semisweet chocolate
- 1/2 cup unsalted butter
- 3/4 cup granulated sugar
- 1/4 teaspoon salt
- 1 teaspoon vanilla extract
- 3 large eggs
- 1/2 cup cocoa powder
- Powdered sugar (for dusting)

Instructions:

1. Preheat oven to 375°F (190°C). Grease an 8-inch round cake pan and line the bottom with parchment paper.
2. Melt chocolate and butter together in a heatproof bowl set over simmering water, stirring occasionally. Once melted, remove from heat and stir in sugar, salt, and vanilla extract.
3. Whisk in eggs one at a time until fully incorporated.
4. Stir in cocoa powder until smooth.
5. Pour the batter into the prepared pan and bake for 20-25 minutes, or until the top is set and a toothpick inserted comes out with a few moist crumbs.
6. Let the cake cool completely, then dust with powdered sugar before serving.

Profiteroles

Ingredients:

- 1 cup water
- 1/2 cup unsalted butter
- 1 teaspoon sugar
- 1/4 teaspoon salt
- 1 cup all-purpose flour
- 4 large eggs
- 1/2 cup heavy cream
- 1 tablespoon powdered sugar
- 1/2 teaspoon vanilla extract

Instructions:

1. Preheat oven to 400°F (200°C). Line a baking sheet with parchment paper.
2. In a saucepan, combine water, butter, sugar, and salt. Bring to a boil over medium heat.
3. Add flour all at once, stirring until the mixture forms a ball and pulls away from the sides of the pan.
4. Remove from heat and let cool for 5 minutes. Add eggs one at a time, stirring after each addition until fully incorporated.
5. Spoon or pipe small mounds of dough onto the prepared baking sheet, leaving space between each.
6. Bake for 20-25 minutes, until puffed and golden brown.
7. While the profiteroles cool, whip heavy cream with powdered sugar and vanilla extract until stiff peaks form.
8. Once cooled, slice the profiteroles in half and fill with whipped cream. Serve immediately.

Chocolate Mousse

Ingredients:

- 8 oz bittersweet chocolate, chopped
- 1 cup heavy cream
- 2 tablespoons powdered sugar
- 1 teaspoon vanilla extract
- 2 large eggs, separated

Instructions:

1. Melt chocolate in a heatproof bowl set over simmering water, stirring until smooth. Let it cool slightly.
2. In a separate bowl, whip heavy cream with powdered sugar and vanilla until stiff peaks form.
3. Beat egg whites in another bowl until soft peaks form.
4. In a separate bowl, whisk egg yolks into the cooled chocolate until combined.
5. Gently fold the whipped cream into the chocolate mixture until smooth.
6. Carefully fold the beaten egg whites into the chocolate mixture until no streaks remain.
7. Spoon the mousse into serving dishes and refrigerate for at least 2 hours before serving.

Salted Caramel Brownies

Ingredients:

- 1/2 cup unsalted butter
- 8 oz bittersweet chocolate
- 3/4 cup granulated sugar
- 3 large eggs
- 1 teaspoon vanilla extract
- 1/2 cup all-purpose flour
- 1/4 teaspoon salt
- 1/2 cup caramel sauce (store-bought or homemade)
- 1/2 teaspoon sea salt

Instructions:

1. Preheat oven to 350°F (175°C). Grease and line an 8x8-inch baking pan with parchment paper.
2. Melt butter and chocolate together in a heatproof bowl set over simmering water.
3. Stir in sugar, eggs, and vanilla extract until combined.
4. Fold in flour and salt until smooth.
5. Pour the batter into the prepared pan and drizzle with caramel sauce.
6. Swirl the caramel into the batter using a knife or skewer.
7. Bake for 25-30 minutes, or until a toothpick inserted comes out with a few moist crumbs.
8. Sprinkle with sea salt before serving.

Mint Chocolate Chip Ice Cream

Ingredients:

- 2 cups heavy cream
- 1 cup whole milk
- 3/4 cup granulated sugar
- 1 teaspoon vanilla extract
- 1 teaspoon peppermint extract
- 1/2 cup mini chocolate chips
- Green food coloring (optional)

Instructions:

1. In a bowl, whisk together heavy cream, milk, sugar, vanilla extract, and peppermint extract until the sugar dissolves.
2. Add a few drops of green food coloring, if desired.
3. Pour the mixture into an ice cream maker and churn according to the manufacturer's instructions.
4. Once the ice cream is thick and creamy, stir in the mini chocolate chips.
5. Transfer the ice cream to a container and freeze for at least 4 hours before serving.

Pumpkin Pie

Ingredients:

- 1 pre-made pie crust
- 1 3/4 cups canned pumpkin puree
- 3/4 cup heavy cream
- 2 large eggs
- 1/2 cup granulated sugar
- 1/2 teaspoon cinnamon
- 1/4 teaspoon ground ginger
- 1/4 teaspoon ground nutmeg
- 1/4 teaspoon salt

Instructions:

1. Preheat oven to 375°F (190°C). Place pie crust in a 9-inch pie dish.
2. In a bowl, whisk together pumpkin, heavy cream, eggs, sugar, cinnamon, ginger, nutmeg, and salt until smooth.
3. Pour the filling into the pie crust.
4. Bake for 45-50 minutes, or until the center is set and a knife inserted comes out clean.
5. Let the pie cool completely before serving.

Almond Cake

Ingredients:

- 1 1/2 cups almond flour
- 1/2 cup all-purpose flour
- 1 teaspoon baking powder
- 1/4 teaspoon salt
- 1/2 cup unsalted butter, softened
- 3/4 cup granulated sugar
- 2 large eggs
- 1 teaspoon vanilla extract
- 1/2 cup whole milk

Instructions:

1. Preheat oven to 350°F (175°C). Grease and line a 9-inch round cake pan with parchment paper.
2. In a bowl, whisk together almond flour, all-purpose flour, baking powder, and salt.
3. In another bowl, cream together butter and sugar until light and fluffy.
4. Beat in eggs one at a time, then add vanilla extract.
5. Gradually add the dry ingredients, alternating with milk, until smooth.
6. Pour the batter into the prepared pan and bake for 25-30 minutes, or until a toothpick inserted comes out clean.
7. Let the cake cool before serving.

Lemon Bars

Ingredients:

- 1 1/2 cups all-purpose flour
- 1/4 cup powdered sugar
- 1/2 cup unsalted butter, softened
- 2 large eggs
- 1 cup granulated sugar
- 1/4 cup lemon juice
- 2 tablespoons all-purpose flour
- Powdered sugar (for dusting)

Instructions:

1. Preheat oven to 350°F (175°C). Grease and line an 8x8-inch baking pan.
2. In a bowl, mix together flour, powdered sugar, and butter until the mixture forms a dough.
3. Press the dough into the bottom of the pan and bake for 15 minutes.
4. While the crust bakes, whisk together eggs, granulated sugar, lemon juice, and flour until smooth.
5. Pour the lemon mixture over the baked crust and return to the oven for 20-25 minutes, until set.
6. Let the bars cool completely, then dust with powdered sugar before serving.

Fruit Sorbet

Ingredients:

- 4 cups fruit (such as berries, mango, or peach)
- 3/4 cup granulated sugar
- 1/2 cup water
- 1 tablespoon lemon juice

Instructions:

1. In a saucepan, combine sugar and water and heat until the sugar dissolves. Let the syrup cool.
2. Puree the fruit in a blender or food processor until smooth.
3. Stir in the cooled syrup and lemon juice.
4. Pour the mixture into an ice cream maker and churn according to the manufacturer's instructions.
5. Transfer to a container and freeze for at least 4 hours before serving.

Chocolate Dipped Strawberries

Ingredients:

- 1 pint fresh strawberries
- 8 oz semisweet or milk chocolate, chopped
- 1/4 cup white chocolate (optional, for drizzling)

Instructions:

1. Wash and dry strawberries thoroughly, leaving the stems on.
2. Melt the semisweet chocolate in a heatproof bowl set over simmering water, stirring until smooth.
3. Dip each strawberry into the melted chocolate, swirling to coat. Place on a parchment-lined baking sheet.
4. If desired, melt white chocolate and drizzle over the dipped strawberries for decoration.
5. Refrigerate the strawberries until the chocolate sets, about 30 minutes.

Fudge

Ingredients:

- 2 cups semisweet chocolate chips
- 1 can (14 oz) sweetened condensed milk
- 2 tablespoons unsalted butter
- 1 teaspoon vanilla extract
- 1/4 teaspoon salt

Instructions:

1. Line an 8-inch square pan with parchment paper.
2. In a saucepan, combine chocolate chips, sweetened condensed milk, butter, and salt. Cook over low heat, stirring constantly until melted and smooth.
3. Remove from heat and stir in vanilla extract.
4. Pour the mixture into the prepared pan and spread evenly.
5. Refrigerate for at least 2 hours or until firm. Cut into squares and serve.

White Chocolate Raspberry Cheesecake

Ingredients:

- 1 1/2 cups graham cracker crumbs
- 1/4 cup sugar
- 1/2 cup unsalted butter, melted
- 2 packages (8 oz each) cream cheese, softened
- 1/2 cup sugar
- 3 large eggs
- 1 teaspoon vanilla extract
- 6 oz white chocolate, chopped
- 1/2 cup raspberry puree
- Fresh raspberries (for garnish)

Instructions:

1. Preheat oven to 325°F (160°C). Grease a 9-inch springform pan.
2. In a bowl, combine graham cracker crumbs, sugar, and melted butter. Press the mixture into the bottom of the pan to form the crust. Bake for 8-10 minutes, then let it cool.
3. In a microwave-safe bowl, melt white chocolate in 30-second intervals, stirring until smooth. Let it cool slightly.
4. In a large bowl, beat cream cheese and sugar until smooth. Add eggs one at a time, beating well after each addition. Stir in vanilla and melted white chocolate.
5. Pour the cream cheese mixture over the crust and smooth the top.
6. Drop spoonfuls of raspberry puree onto the cheesecake batter and swirl with a knife to create a marbled effect.
7. Bake for 55-60 minutes, or until the edges are set and the center is slightly jiggly. Let it cool to room temperature, then refrigerate for at least 4 hours.
8. Garnish with fresh raspberries before serving.

Snickerdoodle Cookies

Ingredients:

- 1 3/4 cups all-purpose flour
- 1/2 teaspoon baking soda
- 1/2 teaspoon cream of tartar
- 1/4 teaspoon salt
- 1/2 cup unsalted butter, softened
- 1 cup sugar
- 2 large eggs
- 1 teaspoon vanilla extract
- 2 tablespoons sugar
- 1 teaspoon ground cinnamon

Instructions:

1. Preheat oven to 350°F (175°C). Line a baking sheet with parchment paper.
2. In a bowl, whisk together flour, baking soda, cream of tartar, and salt.
3. In a large bowl, cream together butter and sugar until light and fluffy. Add eggs one at a time, followed by vanilla extract. Mix in the dry ingredients.
4. In a small bowl, combine cinnamon and sugar. Roll the dough into balls and then roll each ball in the cinnamon-sugar mixture.
5. Place the dough balls on the prepared baking sheet, spacing them about 2 inches apart.
6. Bake for 8-10 minutes, or until golden brown. Let cool on the baking sheet for a few minutes before transferring to a wire rack.

Oatmeal Raisin Cookies

Ingredients:

- 1 cup unsalted butter, softened
- 1 cup brown sugar
- 1/2 cup granulated sugar
- 2 large eggs
- 1 teaspoon vanilla extract
- 1 1/2 cups all-purpose flour
- 1 teaspoon baking soda
- 1/2 teaspoon salt
- 1 1/2 teaspoons cinnamon
- 3 cups old-fashioned oats
- 1 1/2 cups raisins

Instructions:

1. Preheat oven to 350°F (175°C). Line a baking sheet with parchment paper.
2. In a large bowl, cream together butter, brown sugar, and granulated sugar until light and fluffy. Beat in eggs and vanilla extract.
3. In a separate bowl, whisk together flour, baking soda, salt, and cinnamon. Gradually add the dry ingredients to the wet ingredients.
4. Stir in oats and raisins.
5. Drop spoonfuls of dough onto the prepared baking sheet, spacing them about 2 inches apart.
6. Bake for 10-12 minutes, or until golden brown. Let cool on the baking sheet for a few minutes before transferring to a wire rack.

Chocoflan

Ingredients:

- 1/2 cup sugar (for caramel)
- 1 box (18.25 oz) chocolate cake mix
- 1 can (12 oz) evaporated milk
- 1 can (14 oz) sweetened condensed milk
- 3 large eggs
- 1 teaspoon vanilla extract
- 1/4 teaspoon salt

Instructions:

1. Preheat oven to 350°F (175°C). Grease a 9-inch round cake pan.
2. In a small saucepan, melt sugar over medium heat until golden brown. Immediately pour the melted sugar into the prepared cake pan and swirl to coat the bottom.
3. Prepare the chocolate cake mix according to package instructions. Pour the cake batter into the pan over the caramel.
4. In a blender, combine evaporated milk, sweetened condensed milk, eggs, vanilla extract, and salt. Pour the milk mixture carefully over the cake batter.
5. Place the cake pan in a larger baking dish and fill the outer dish with hot water to create a water bath.
6. Bake for 1 hour, or until the cake is set. Let it cool, then refrigerate for at least 2 hours.
7. Run a knife around the edge of the cake and invert onto a plate to serve.

Toffee Pudding

Ingredients:

- 1 1/2 cups all-purpose flour
- 1 teaspoon baking powder
- 1/4 teaspoon salt
- 1/2 cup unsalted butter, softened
- 1/2 cup packed brown sugar
- 1 large egg
- 1 teaspoon vanilla extract
- 1 cup boiling water
- 1/2 cup heavy cream
- 1/4 cup toffee sauce (store-bought or homemade)

Instructions:

1. Preheat oven to 350°F (175°C). Grease a 9-inch baking dish.
2. In a bowl, whisk together flour, baking powder, and salt.
3. In a separate bowl, cream together butter and brown sugar. Beat in egg and vanilla extract.
4. Gradually add the dry ingredients, mixing until just combined.
5. Pour the batter into the prepared baking dish. Carefully pour the boiling water over the batter.
6. Bake for 30-35 minutes, or until the top is golden and bubbly.
7. In a saucepan, heat heavy cream and toffee sauce over medium heat until warmed through.
8. Pour the toffee sauce over the warm pudding and serve.

Coconut Cream Pie

Ingredients:

- 1 pre-made pie crust
- 1 cup sugar
- 1/2 cup cornstarch
- 1/4 teaspoon salt
- 4 large egg yolks
- 2 1/2 cups whole milk
- 1/2 cup unsweetened shredded coconut
- 1 teaspoon vanilla extract
- 1 tablespoon butter
- Whipped cream (for topping)

Instructions:

1. Preheat oven to 350°F (175°C). Bake the pie crust according to package instructions.
2. In a saucepan, combine sugar, cornstarch, and salt. Whisk in egg yolks and milk. Cook over medium heat, whisking constantly, until thickened.
3. Remove from heat and stir in shredded coconut, vanilla extract, and butter.
4. Pour the mixture into the baked pie crust. Let it cool to room temperature, then refrigerate for at least 4 hours.
5. Top with whipped cream before serving.

Spiced Pear Cake

Ingredients:

- 1 1/2 cups all-purpose flour
- 1 teaspoon baking soda
- 1/2 teaspoon cinnamon
- 1/4 teaspoon ground ginger
- 1/4 teaspoon salt
- 1/2 cup unsalted butter, softened
- 1 cup brown sugar
- 2 large eggs
- 2 pears, peeled and diced
- 1/2 cup chopped walnuts (optional)

Instructions:

1. Preheat oven to 350°F (175°C). Grease and line an 8-inch round cake pan.
2. In a bowl, whisk together flour, baking soda, cinnamon, ginger, and salt.
3. In another bowl, cream together butter and brown sugar. Beat in eggs one at a time.
4. Gradually add the dry ingredients, mixing until combined.
5. Fold in diced pears and walnuts, if using.
6. Pour the batter into the prepared cake pan and bake for 35-40 minutes, or until a toothpick inserted comes out clean.
7. Let the cake cool before serving.

www.ingramcontent.com/pod-product-compliance
Lightning Source LLC
LaVergne TN
LVHW081505060526
838201LV00056BA/2934